ANIMATION

Written by
Janine Amos

Illustrated by
Kim Lane

Consultant Editor
Stan Hayward

Collins

CONTENTS

Making it move

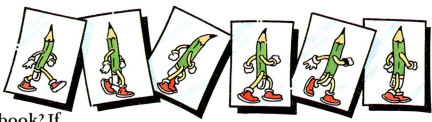

Have you ever made a flip book? If you have, you're an animator. You can animate! You can make still pictures appear to move.

A cartoon film is made up of thousands of still pictures. Each picture is called a *frame* (technical words like this are in italics, and there is more about them on page 30). Each frame shows a slightly different movement. They flash past your eyes so quickly that they don't look still at all. Instead, they seem to make up one continuous movement.

An enormous amount of work goes into the making of even the shortest animated film. It takes a whole team of skilled people and a wide range of specialized equipment. It also takes a long time. But it's worth it – for how else could you make a pencil walk or an elephant fly?

Flip trick

Use a small notebook or staple some blank pieces of paper together to make a book.

Starting at the top right of the first page, draw a figure in one stage of a movement – like running, diving or kicking a football. Press quite hard with your pencil.

On the next page, trace over the marks your pencil made but change your figure very slightly in some way. Go on doing this through to the end of the book.

We have made this book into a flip book too. Flip through the pages and you'll see the green bean jump into the air!

Now flip through the pages with your thumb – and watch your still pictures 'move'!

A STAR IS BORN

All the animated films you have ever seen probably began in the same place! The chances are that they all began around a table, with a group of people in deep discussion.

Writer   Client   Producer

The group probably included a *producer* – the person in charge of the smooth running of the film – a *writer* and a *client*. The client is the customer who will pay for the film to be made. And the writer writes. She does a lot more besides: she must decide on the type of film the client wants, dream up the characters and work out the story. Then she must communicate all this to a *designer*, who will draw the characters.

This client wants a new cartoon series for children's television. He discusses ideas with the producer and the writer. The producer is concerned with the cost of the film and the time it will take to make. The writer is concerned with the age of the viewers. She makes lots of notes about what the client wants.

The writer researches ideas and types out suggestions. She usually works alone, outside the studio. One of the most important jobs for the writer is to decide upon the personalities of the characters in her stories. She has to imagine how they will behave when all kinds of things happen to them.

After a lot of discussion between the client and the producer, and a great deal of hard work by the writer and designer, a new character is in the making. And, sometimes, a star is born!

The writer types suggestions.

When the writer is happy with her ideas, she gives them to the designer. The designer will produce some rough drawings of the characters and their backgrounds. She needs as much information as possible from the writer – the kinds of clothes a character will wear, how he walks and how he sits down, for example.

Sometimes the writer will act out the character for the designer!

The writer poses for the designer.

The designer then draws the characters on *model sheets*. Model sheets give all the information about the characters, such as their personalities, moods and emotions, and views of them from every angle. The drawings also show the characters in various positions – walking, running, climbing, sitting.

The designer's model sheet

The designer draws the characters from all angles.

THE MODEL SHEET

All model sheets are different.
They depend on the designer and
the character she's drawing. But they
all show certain things.

First of all, they
show what the
character looks
like. They also
give details of the
character's
proportions. For
example, the
head may be one
third the size of
the whole body.

6

The model sheet may also show the sizes of one character compared with another.

The model sheet is also a guide to how the character will move. *Postures* and *gestures* must be shown at this stage.

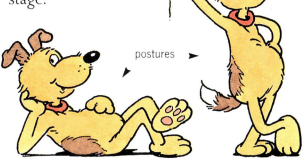

postures ▶

◀ gestures ▶

The designer works out a series of moods and expressions for characters.

happy

sad

cross

Clothes are matched to the personalities of characters.

Props, like umbrellas, handbags or swords can say a lot about a character.

DRAWING THE STORYBOARD

Using the written script and the model sheet, the designer draws up the *storyboard*. It will be the basis of the whole film. The storyboard is like a comic strip. It contains the characters' speech, called the *dialogue*, the action and the basic camera instructions. It will be used as a working guide by all the people in the animation team.

The storyboard shows the actions which make up every scene in the film. The designer makes notes on the storyboard to indicate camera movements. She uses words like cut and fade. On the storyboard on the right and in the yellow box on the opposite page you can find out what some of these words mean.

At the zoo, dog speaks to zoo keeper.

Keeper: What can I do for you?
ZOOM IN ON DOG & KEEPER

Dog: It's my birthday. Do you have room for a party?

KEEPER LOOKS PUZZLED. HAS IDEA.

PAN ACROSS. STOP AT GIRAFFE.
They visit enclosures. Giraffe can't help.

CUT TO LION.
Lion: You can join us if you like.

The layout artist then produces a *layout*. This gives an overall view of the scene of the action. It will be used as a guide by the animator and the background artist.

CUT TO DOG.

Dog: Ehm, no thank you.

ZOOM OUT FROM DOG.

Dog returns to his friend.

MIX RABBIT.

Dog: There's no room for a party at the zoo.

Rabbit: What'll we do?.

CUT TO CLOSE-UP.

Dog: I've got an idea!

Cut: A direct change of scene – from one shot to another.

Fade: The picture slowly changes to black – it fades out.

Mix: Fading out one scene but fading on another at the same time.

Zoom: A movement in or out – for example towards a face – to give a close-up shot – or away from a face.

THE RECORDING STUDIO

It's time to record the voice, which is called the *voicetrack*. The script for the voicetrack is taken from the storyboard. This happens under the guidance of a *director*. He explains to the actors the kinds of voices he wants for the characters.

The character's speech is called *dialogue*. The director may do several versions of the recording and choose the best one later.

The recording engineer

Recording the voicetrack.

A *recording engineer* records the voicetrack and transfers it to sprocketted magnetic tape. Sprockets are square holes along the edge of the tape. They allow sound on the tape to be matched with the picture on the film. The tape is then passed to the *editor* along with the storyboard. Using a machine called a *synchroniser* he breaks down the voicetrack into small sections to fit the storyboard and the actions of the characters.

A dial on the synchroniser records the length of every sound. Sounds are timed in frames – the individual pictures which make up the film. Each frame lasts 1/24th of a second and the editor shows where each sound begins and ends. This is put on to a *dopesheet* and passed to the animator. The animator can now match her drawings exactly to the sounds. The dopesheet also shows where the action begins and ends.

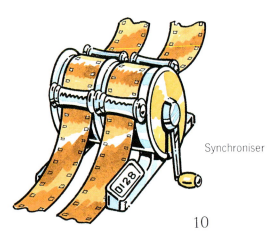

Synchroniser

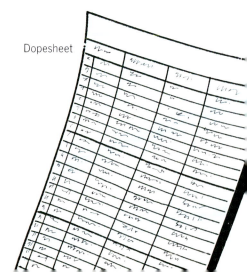

Dopesheet

The music *composer* also needs to know when the action, dialogue and sound effects start and stop, so that he can write music to fit the scene. He uses a simple type of dopesheet to guide him, called a *barsheet*.

The music is recorded on a music track. The sound effects are put in last. They are recorded on a separate sound effects track.

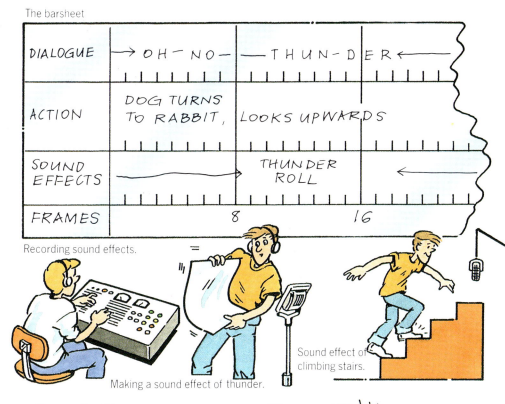

The barsheet

DIALOGUE	→ OH ‒ NO ‒	‒ T H U N ‒ D ER ←	
ACTION	DOG TURNS TO RABBIT,	LOOKS UPWARDS	
SOUND EFFECTS		THUNDER ROLL	←
FRAMES	8	16	

Recording sound effects.

Making a sound effect of thunder.

Sound effect of climbing stairs.

Sound effects to try yourself

Try making a flip book of a man caught in a storm and record your own sound effects to go with it! Baking trays or a large sheet of cardboard may give you some realistic thunderclaps. You could also try a running figure (run on the spot on small stones in a washing-up bowl) or an underwater scene (blow through a straw into a bowl of water). Noises like *crash*, *bang*, *wallop*, *thud*, *splosh* and *hiss* are also fun to make.

Underwater sounds

Tape recorder and microphone

Paddling sounds

Thunder

11

THE ANIMATOR

The animator is a special kind of artist. While most artists are interested in shapes and colours, the animator is mainly interested in movement.

Before the animator begins her sketches she needs the storyboards and the layouts. They show her how the character fits into the background and the sort of action required.

Storyboard

Model sheet

Rough sketches

Dopesheet

She also needs the dopesheet, showing how long the action and the dialogue take, and the model sheet, showing how the character looks in different positions.

Quite often she will listen to a cassette of the soundtrack to get a feeling of the character's mood.

Now the animator gives movement to the mood. The designer who drew the model sheet was concerned with the character's appearance. The animator is concerned with the character's movement.

Habits like walks and gestures help to show personality. The story may ask for a happy walk.

Or the character may have to hang his head and slouch unhappily along the road.

The animator asks herself questions like: Is it a fast walk, or a run? Do his arms swing?

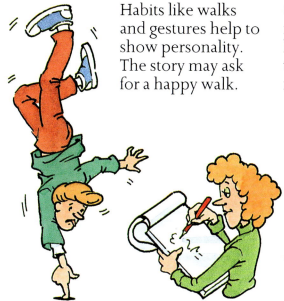

The animator decides the best way for her character to walk to show his personality and his mood. She may ask someone to act out the movements while she makes notes and sketches.

The animator shows the character's personality through his movements.

She may invent little extras which add to the feeling she is trying to create.

When the animator has decided how her character will move, she is ready to start on her drawings, scene by scene.

THE ANIMATOR'S ASSISTANT

Find yourself a glass of lemonade, sit at a table and raise the glass to your mouth. Now think about the movement your arm made. Did it have a beginning, a middle and an end? This line of thought is all in a day's work for an animator. The job of animation is all about breaking movements down into many different parts, and putting them together again!

The animator uses the dopesheet from the editor to see how long each sound takes. She will make her drawings fit the sound. Then she sketches all the positions needed to make one movement.

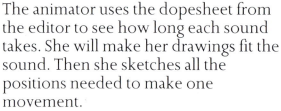

Animator sketch

Now the animator begins to make her *key drawings*. These are the first and last drawings of every movement her character makes.

Key drawings

The animator puts a note on the paper of exactly how many movements come in between her key drawings.

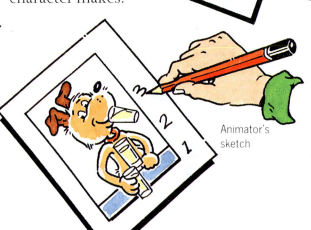

Animator's sketch

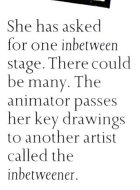

She has asked for one *inbetween* stage. There could be many. The animator passes her key drawings to another artist called the *inbetweener*.

He makes as many inbetween drawings as the animator has asked for. Here is his inbetween stage of the movement:

Inbetween drawing

To save time, the drawings are made up of several pieces of clear plastic, called *cels*, one on top of another. Only the *action* part of the drawing needs to be redrawn each time. For the lemonade scene, a head, body and three sets of arms are needed.

Peg holes

 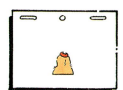 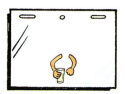  

Cels of the dog's movements

All the drawings have peg holes at the top so they can fit over each other exactly. The drawings are changed on top of the background.

Pegs

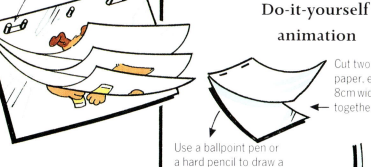

Do-it-yourself animation

Cut two strips of thin paper, each about 8cm wide. Staple them together at the top.

Use a ballpoint pen or a hard pencil to draw a face on the top piece of paper. Draw a happy mouth on the top piece.

Now trace over the marks on your bottom piece of paper – but change the mouth to a sad one.

When each scene has been drawn all the drawings are shot in order on video instead of film. This is called a *line test* and it's just like a rehearsal. The animator checks to see if any movement looks too slow or jerky. If it is, she can make the changes before the drawings are coloured in.

Start at the bottom of the top piece of paper and roll it tightly around your pencil. When you take the pencil away the paper will curl by itself. Use your pencil to flip the top paper – and watch your drawing appear to 'move'.

The animator checks all the movements.

IN THE BACKGROUND

Imagine a spotted dog in a field of daisies. You might not see much of the dog! Backgrounds may be bright, dull, simple or full of detail. But they must not draw attention away from the characters. While the animator and the inbetweener are working on the figures, other artists are busy creating backgrounds to suit each scene of the film.

The background artist uses the layout as a guide for the background drawings.

Background with character

Peg bar holes

Cel overlay

Painting of background only

Background and cel combined

There are two types of background – a still background and a moving one. With a still background, only the characters move.

Moving backgrounds are often used to show things like cars travelling along roads. In fact, the car doesn't move at all – it's the background that moves behind it! Other artists work on *effects*. They are good at creating things like rain, snow, explosions or water. When these are placed in front of the animated characters they are called *foreground* effects.

Some artists specialize in lettering or the titles at the beginning of a film.

Background for moving scene

Cel of dog walking

Dog superimposed over
moving background

Snow

Rain

Smoke

SHOOT!

Tracing and painting.

Painting the cels.

Checking the dopesheet.

When the animation of each scene is finished, the drawings are passed to the _trace and paint artists._ They trace the drawings from paper on to clear plastic cels.

Cels allow the background to show through. This means you can put one drawing over another and see what is happening underneath. The paint is put on to the back of each cel. The colour shines through, making the paint look flat and even. The artists working on trace and paint usually wear thin cotton gloves – any fingermarks on the cel will show up later under the camera lights.

When all the work has been finished by the animators, inbetweeners, background artists and trace and painters, it is sent to the _checker._ She makes sure that the pictures are all in order and properly noted down on the dopesheet. Then everything is passed to the _cameraman._

18

Using the dopesheet, the cameraman photographs the cels in the right order and works out the camera movements. He uses an animation camera called a *rostrum camera* which photographs one frame at a time. The camera can be moved closer or farther away from the cels so that it can shoot all or part of the picture. The cels can be moved sideways frame by frame to create movement. To shoot each frame, the cameraman presses a button.

The rostrum camera

Shooting the frames.

19

PICTURE AND SOUND

The final stage in the animation process involves someone called the *editor* who matches picture with sound.

When the cameraman has shot the film he sends it to the laboratories to be developed. This produces a *negative*, and from the negative a copy called a print is made. The negative is kept in a safe place until later. The editor cuts the print and fits it to the soundtrack of the film. This print is called the *cutting copy*.

The editor puts the cutting copy on to the synchroniser with the voicetrack and cuts the film so that it matches up exactly.

Then he puts the music track on to the synchroniser and matches that up.

Negative

Cutting copy

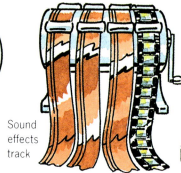
Sound effects track

Finally he matches up the sound effects. He can now run the film with all three soundtracks together.

Now the sounds are mixed balancing their volumes so they do not clash with each other. This is recorded on to a fresh piece of sprocketted magnetic film. This work is done in a *dubbing theatre*.

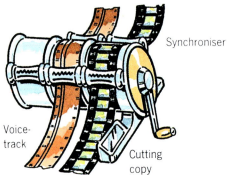
Synchroniser

Voice-track

Cutting copy

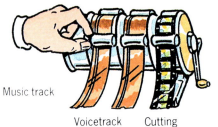
Music track

Voicetrack

Cutting copy

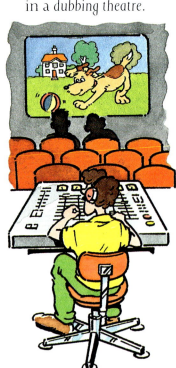
The dubbing theatre

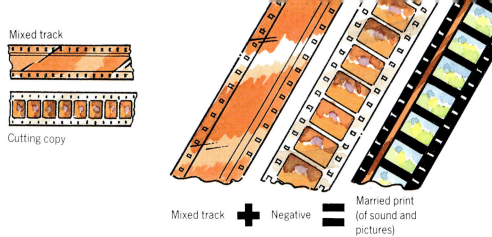

Mixed track

Cutting copy

Mixed track **+** Negative **=** Married print (of sound and pictures)

First the film is run with the voicetrack. The volume is made loud and soft where necessary. Then the music and sound effects tracks are added. This is called *mixing.* The editor makes sure that they are all the right volume and do not interfere with the voicetrack.

The mixed track is then sent to the laboratory with the editor's cutting copy. The laboratory uses the cutting copy of the film as a guide to cut the negative for the master film. A film of the soundtrack is made and printed alongside the master negative on a fresh piece of film to make the *married print* of sound and pictures.

The film is now complete! The negative is used to make lots of copies to be sent to all the cinemas and TV companies. If the film is to be used on TV, it is now transferred to video tape, as this is easier to use than film.

A video tape of the film is shown to the client.

PAPER, PAINT AND PUPPETS

You can animate anything! Pencils and rubbers can go racing across a desk top, dolls can dance, and screws can twist themselves out of a plank of wood – and back in again!

There are three main kinds of animation – *drawn, cut-out* and *model animation*. All animation comes under one of these headings.

Drawn animation covers any form of animation where the 'movement' is made by a new drawing. Cel animation and drawing in sand or with string are examples of this.

Cels

A sand figure

A string drawing

Cut-out animation is usually quicker and cheaper than drawn animation. Hinged figures and characters are cut from magazines or photographs and are moved by hand between camera shots.

Cut-outs for the eyes, mouth, ears and hands of a hinged figure.

Models made out of latex, and moved bit by bit for the animated sequence.

Model animation covers the movement of 3D objects, like puppets, dolls and models made from wood, latex, wax or Plasticine.

They can be made to do things which can never happen in real life!

The strip of film shows the movement frame by frame.

This series of pictures shows how everyday objects and materials like paint powders, spoons and forks can be used to make animated models. This kind of animation is often used in advertising.

Simple models can be made from everyday objects like paint powders.

Paper, toys, spoons and forks are used for these animated sequences.

MAKING MODELS MOVE

Models are animated by moving their arms, legs, bodies and faces very, very slightly in between each camera shot. Just as in drawn animation where the action of drinking a glass of lemonade was made up of several drawings, in model animation the model's arm would be moved, bit by bit, many times.

The animator poses the model's arm, then takes one camera shot.

The model's arm is moved again and another shot is taken.

The final shot. Seconds of screen time may take hours of work.

When the shots are run one after another, the models appear to be moving smoothly.

Animated models must be simple figures since they have to be handled between every shot. Sometimes arms or legs drop off and the animator must remodel another figure exactly like the first. Several models may be made and swapped instead of repaired.

Dick Spanner, the animated detective hero created by Gerry Anderson.

Table-top animation has a world of its own – in miniature. The scenery, or set, in which the model moves often takes hours to build. The animator creates a miniature world for the characters on a table top.

The models in their table-top worlds.

Models created for a pop video by Aardman Animations.

SPECIAL EFFECTS

How does your favourite actor turn into a werewolf? And how does a giant gorilla wreck a city? Animation is used in many ways to create the impossible on television and for the cinema.

Live action films use live people and animated films use puppet or cartoon people, but there are many kinds of films where both are mixed. This often happens in science fiction stories, horror and comedy films, when surprising things go on which could never happen in real life. These films use special effects.

Animated models are sometimes used to film disasters like earthquakes. Real actors may be filmed in front of projected backgrounds.

A model background of an earthquake.

To turn an actor into a wolf-man, animation is used to make the changes. It takes hours for the make-up to be applied and for each stage to be photographed, a frame at a time. On film it seems to take only a few seconds for the change to take place.

This sequence shows how a make-up artist transforms an actor making him look like a wolf-man.

A real actor in front of a projected background.

26

Animation and live action are often combined, especially in commercials. The live action is filmed with actors pretending to see the animated characters. The film is then projected on to a glass screen one frame at a time. The animator draws the characters to match the film.

To make the character jump down from the cereal packet, animation is carried out after live action.

Sometimes models are used along with the real thing. A wild animal may be filmed but replaced in certain scenes by an animated model. In this way, close-up shots can show the animal doing something which it might take months to film in real life.

The model squirrel can be moved into various positions.

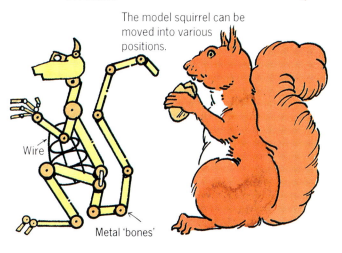

Wire

Metal 'bones'

Live action scene of actor and real squirrel.

Actor stroking the tail of the animated model squirrel.

Now imagine an actor fighting a three-headed monster! The 'monster' may be a small animated model. But for close-up shots a larger model is made. By moving the camera from a small model to a large head, it seems as if the actor really is battling with a huge creature.

Small model of the monster is animated.

Close-up of the monster uses just the heads.

COMPUTERS IN ANIMATION

Computers are used by animation studios to speed up the production process. And some types of computer can also be used to produce exciting special effects.

Computer generated images.

Many of the titles you see on television programmes or at the cinema are produced by computer. Letters may be coloured, curved into 3D forms, they may wave, shimmer or flash. Sometimes the title melts into the picture or dances in front of an image.

A drawing of a frog which was made into a 3D model for computer animation.

A "wire-frame" computer drawing made from the 3D model.

The completed computer drawing ready to be used for animation.

Computer animation of sweets turning into a face.

The face changes its expression in a close-up.

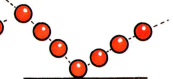

Here the sweets are dancing with each other.

Computers can't replace the animator's skill in working out a character's postures and gestures, but they can help with inbetweening and timing.

An animator can make the bouncing ball look squashed.

A computer can time the sequence of bounces very accurately, but the movement isn't as realistic.

Computers can also work out accurate and complicated paths for the animated figures or objects to follow.

Computers are very often used for the special effects in science fiction films. Spacecraft can be made to fly very fast through small gaps between buildings. Other objects, like flying saucers, can be made to rotate as they move along.

A computer-generated picture made for a satellite TV company.

Spin animation!

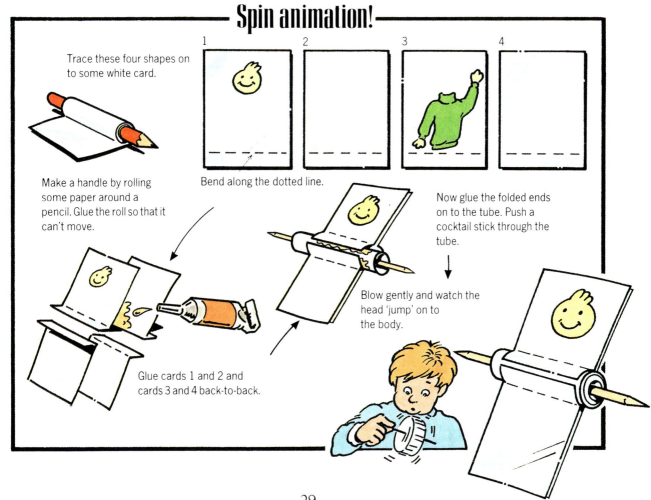

Trace these four shapes on to some white card.

Make a handle by rolling some paper around a pencil. Glue the roll so that it can't move.

Bend along the dotted line.

1 2 3 4

Glue cards 1 and 2 and cards 3 and 4 back-to-back.

Now glue the folded ends on to the tube. Push a cocktail stick through the tube.

Blow gently and watch the head 'jump' on to the body.

THE FUTURE

It is becoming more and more difficult to say where animation ends and live action begins! In the future it is likely that more animation techniques will be used in areas such as teaching, advertising and spectacular entertainment films.

Just as cinema films have soundtracks, it is now common for pop songs to have pictures put to them. These pop videos often use animation combined with live action. In the future, you might make an animated movie to send to someone, instead of a letter or a card!

New electronic techniques and sophisticated systems for use with animation are being introduced all the time. But the art of animation will always be in the hands of the animator. In a business which changes daily, it is hard to predict the future. Yet one thing is for sure – animation, which began long before live action films were made, has a long way to go before all its possibilities have been explored.

Animated television commercials are often at the forefront of technical developments. You might like to keep an eye out for these kinds of animations.

GLOSSARY

Action	The movement in the film. The action part of the drawing is the part that is moving.
Animation	Any form of recording on film or video that shoots one frame at a time. The objects are still at the time of shooting.
Cel/drawn animation	The type of animation that uses drawings.
Computer animation	This uses computers to do the animation instead of an animator. It is very good for technical effects but not so good for animating people and animals.
Cut-out animation	The type of animation that uses cut-out shapes instead of drawings.
Model animation	This uses 3D models and figures.
Special effects animation	This uses animation combined with live action film. It is often seen in horror, science fiction or comedy films.
Animator	The artist who decides how the character will move, and who prepares the key drawings.
Background	Moving background – a long scene which is moved behind the characters to make them look as though they are moving. Still background – a still scene which is behind the moving characters.
Barsheet	A simple form of the dopesheet, often used by the composer.
Camera instructions	Written instructions from the animator to the cameraman. They are usually written on the storyboard. Some of the basic instructions are:
cut	A direct change of scene, from one shot to another.
fade	To fade a picture out, usually to black, as at the end of a scene.
mix	To fade one picture out while fading a new one on.
zoom	To move in towards one part of the picture for a close-up shot.
Cel	Short for cellulose acetate film – the clear plastic sheet on to which the final drawings are traced for painting.

Checker	The person who checks the drawings and makes sure they are in order before they go to the cameraman.		an overall view of the scene of the action. It is used as a guide by the animator and the background artist.
Client	The person who pays the animation studio to make the film.	Line test	A test shot using the animator's and the inbetweener's pencil drawings to check movement and timing.
Composer	The person who creates the music.	Married print	The final film, which includes sound and picture.
Cutting copy	The copy of the film which the laboratory sends to the editor to cut and fit to the soundtrack.	Mixing	Putting the voicetrack, music track and the sound effects on to one soundtrack.
Designer	The artist who is concerned with the look of the character and the backgrounds.	Model sheet	The designer's character drawings, showing the gestures, shape, colour, size and proportions of the character.
Dialogue	The characters' speech.	Posture	The way a character stands or holds himself in position, for example with hands on hips.
Director	The person responsible for everything that appears on the final film.		
Dopesheet	The instruction sheet on to which the editor puts the soundtrack information for the animator, and on to which the animator puts the camera instructions for the cameraman.	Producer	The person responsible for delivering the finished film to the clients on time, and for making sure it is as they wanted.
		Prop	Any article, like an umbrella, sword or piece of equipment used by a character.
Dubbing theatre	The studio where the soundtracks are balanced and mixed to the picture.	Recording engineer	The person who operates the recording equipment which records the soundtracks.
Editor	The person who matches picture with sound to make the final film.	Rostrum camera	The special camera used for animation.
Foreground	Trees and other objects in front of the characters.	Soundtrack	Any track which includes sound – the voicetrack, the music track or the sound effects, or all of these combined on a single track.
Foreground effects	Effects like rain, snow, water and explosions which are drawn on to a cel and placed over the drawings of the characters.		
Frame	A single picture of the film.	Storyboard	The plan of the film as drawings, showing the dialogue, action and basic camera movements.
Gesture	An arm or body movement which reflects the character's personality or mood.	Synchroniser	A set of cogged wheels over which the film and soundtracks can be wound to allow pictures and sounds to be matched together.
Inbetweens	All the drawings which go between the key drawings to make a movement.		
Key drawings	The animator's drawings of the beginning and end positions in a movement.	Trace and painter	The artist who traces the animator's and the inbetweener's pencil drawings on to cel, and paints them.
Layout	The designer's drawing which gives		

INDEX

Acknowledgements
The publishers would like to thank the following for their assistance in the preparation of this book and for permission to reproduce copyright material: Aardman Animations Ltd, cover (bottom), page 23 (top left and right), 25 (bottom left and right); Anderson Burr Partnership (Gerry Anderson, Terry Adlam), page 24, 25 (top left and right); Gill Bradley and Snapper Films, page 23 (bottom); IMAGINE, page 29; Robinson Lambie-Nairn Ltd, cover (top and middle), page 28.

ISBN 0 00 190017 X (Hardback)
ISBN 0 00 190075 7 (Paperback)

A CIP catalogue record for this book is available from the British Library

William Collins Sons & Co Ltd.
London · Glasgow · Sydney · Auckland
Toronto · Johannesburg

First published in Great Britain 1990
© William Collins Sons & Co Ltd

Printed and bound in Singapore by Kim Hup Lee Printing Co. Pte. Ltd.